DISCIPLINE
Made Easy

TIPS AND TECHNIQUES FOR
CATHOLIC SCHOOL TEACHERS AND CATECHISTS

The author, obviously an experienced catechist herself, offers a host of practical ideas for setting up the conditions that promote a balance of order and comfort in the classroom environment."

—David M. Riley
The Catechist

"Sr. Kathleen concludes *Discipline Made Easy* with a list of beatitudes for religion teachers. I add another: Happy are the religion teachers who read this book, for they are certain to find many valuable tips to improve their teaching.

—Dr. Tom Walters
Emeritus professor,
Saint Meinrad School of Theology

"*Discipline Made Easy* is the book I've been looking for since I became a DRE! Discipline is the one issue that hounds most veteran teachers and terrifies most prospective ones. Time and time again, they have asked me for resources to assist them in the area of discipline. DREs now have a valuable resource to offer.

—Joe Paprocki
Author, *The Catechist's Toolbox*
and *Beyond the Catechist's Toolbox*

DISCIPLINE
Made Easy

Tips and Techniques for
Catholic School Teachers and Catechists

Mary Kathleen Glavich, SND

National Catholic Educational Association

Copyright © 2017 by the National Catholic Educational Association, 1005 N. Glebe Rd., Suite 525, Arlington, VA 22201. All rights reserved, including the right of reproduction in whole or part in any form. Published in the United States of America by the National Catholic Educational Association. www.NCEA.org

ISBN: 978-1-55833-620-9

Part No.: REL-30-1567

TABLE OF CONTENTS

INTRODUCTION

Whoever seeks God must accept discipline.
—Sirach 32:14 (New American Bible)

At a faculty meeting at the beginning of the school year, the Director of Religious Education (DRE) introduced Judy, a new catechist. Out of the goodness of her heart, Judy had consented to fill a vacancy in the final hour and teach the sixth grade. Judy stood to acknowledge our applause. Then she pleaded, "I'm petrified. I'm afraid I won't have discipline. Can anyone help me?"

Judy was right to be concerned about discipline. With the change of one word, 1 Corinthians 13:1 becomes a truism for teachers: "If I speak in the tongues of mortals and of angels, but do not have discipline, I am a noisy gong or a clanging cymbal." A's in methods courses, expensive audiovisuals, and hours of preparation are all worthless unless students cooperate. Discipline is essential for teaching. We teachers cajole, coerce, and dazzle children into allowing education to happen. Inability to maintain discipline is the main reason teachers quit. Luckily, discipline is a skill that can be learned, and it can improve with practice. There are strategies that can turn an undisciplined class into a model class.

This book is for new teachers like Judy who are wondering how they will ever manage a class of rambunctious youngsters and teach them something. It is also for teachers who are experiencing major or minor difficulties with discipline. It might even offer seasoned educators a fresh idea or two to try out this year or give them a new insight into the art of teaching.

In compiling material for this book, I asked several teachers for ideas. One friend replied, "Discipline in religion class? That's easy. All you need is a whip and a chair." I hope you find the suggestions in this book much more practical and helpful for your ministry.

The meaning of discipline

It is no mere coincidence that *disciple* and *discipline* share the same root word: the Latin word *dicere*, which means "to learn." Our students are disciples, learners. Would that they were as spellbound as Jesus' disciples. When he taught, crowds followed him across lakes and into deserts. They even forgot about eating! Some days we're lucky if our students just look attentive.

Discipline is basically a situation that is conducive to learning. It allows all the disciple's energy to be focused on learning. The student is motivated to learn, not to misbehave. Discipline sets the stage for success, and success is the best motivator.

Teachers facilitate classroom discipline by managing the physical arrangement and setting the climate for optimum learning to occur. The goal of this external discipline, however, is self-discipline on the part of the students. Self-discipline, or self-control, enables students to hear and absorb the truths and skills we are teaching. It is self-discipline, too, that enables them to live according to the Gospel.

By teaching with good discipline and ultimately teaching self-discipline, we are preparing the children we teach for the Christian life. We are helping them to live like Jesus. With self-discipline they will be better equipped to do these things:

- Listen to others who have different opinions
- Survive trials, pain, and suffering
- Persevere through unexpected setbacks
- Sacrifice for the sake of love—live the way of the cross
- Speak out against injustice
- Bite their tongues when sarcastic comments are on the tip of them
- Live immune to materialism and consumerism
- Reach out to the poor, the suffering, and those who are in distress
- Get up to celebrate the Eucharist when their bodies crave to stay in a warm, cozy bed.

Clearly, establishing good classroom discipline has far-reaching repercussions in the lives of those we teach. Unfortunately, achieving it today is more of a challenge than ever.

Why students won't behave

Teaching today's children is especially difficult and frequently frustrating because of discipline problems. A fourth-grade catechist reports that her students are so unmanageable that all she can do with them is sing! That in itself is an accomplishment. Another teacher says that her seventh graders think everything is a joke. Teachers find obscenities on the board, graffiti carved into student desks, and broken equipment. One first-year high school teacher discovered that her car tires were slashed. No wonder there is a high dropout rate among us.

Our Culture

First of all, society complicates our task by teaching and endorsing values contrary to the Gospel values we teach. By the time children are sitting in our classrooms, many have already adopted neo-pagan attitudes and practices, not only from the media but from their friends, neighbors, and families. As the *National Catechetical Directory* points out, "Many Catholics are poorly informed about their faith or have deliberately rejected parts of it" (24). We might just as well be from Mars when we teach that premarital sex is wrong or that self-denial is a good thing. Often, if what we have to say is not denied outright or challenged, it is simply tolerated by those we teach.

Families on the Move

Another factor is the high rate of mobility in the United States, which leaves little chance for a family or child to sink roots in a faith community and be nurtured by it. For most Catholic families, the parish is no longer the center of family life. Only about thirty percent of Catholic families go to Mass. In many cases, then, the concepts, rituals, and vocabulary of a Catholic school are foreign to the children. Moreover, as the children transfer from school to school, the development of a subject's curriculum is piecemeal.

Family Circumstances

Other facts that explain less-than-angelic behavior are related to family life. Too many children are from disturbed or broken families and families that are facing emotional or financial problems. Learning is difficult if not impossible. Many Catholic families are now headed by a single parent who probably works.

And, in a large percentage of two-parent homes, both parents work. Many children who are left alone for extended periods of time are engrossed in video games or television shows. Some television values are questionable at best. And because today's media are highly entertaining, children expect to be entertained in school, too.

Then, too, often "latchkey" children are accustomed to being their own bosses. They resent being told what to do. Naturally, when we take a stand against the wishes of these children, conflict is the result. In the past, when children were reprimanded in school, parents would follow through at home. Today they tend to defend their offspring and ask why the teacher is picking on their child.

Non-Catholic Students

Particularly in inner-city and changing neighborhoods, the number of non-Catholic children in Catholic schools is growing. A few of these students who do not see the need for learning the Catholic faith and participating in Catholic traditions may cause problems.

Less Respect

Children treat authority figures differently today in general. Though it is a positive thing not to fear adults and those in charge, it is quite another thing to be disrespectful. Parents often unwittingly allow children to confuse lack of fear with lack of respect. In one of my classes, fourteen-year-old Susie was particularly disrespectful. When I called her mother, I could hear Susie yelling in the background. "Is she fighting with her brothers?" I asked. "No," sighed the mother, "she's talking to me. I don't know what to do with her."

In the light of all of these situations, student misbehavior in class is understandable. But being understandable doesn't make it acceptable. Our goal should be to establish good discipline: a climate conducive to learning and growth.

Don't get discouraged or give up

Children are in your class to learn, and one item of your hidden curriculum is discipline. As we have seen, many children do not come programmed to listen, follow directions, share, cooperate, and communicate. Often you have to instill proper behavior by untiringly calling them to it. When the class is restless and talking, instead of raising your voice to carry over the commotion, stop and deal with the problem. When George yells out for the hundredth time, correct him for the hundredth time.

Once during a school Mass, while a student was drinking from the cup, the boy behind her quipped, "Hey, leave some for us!" After Mass I captured the boy and roundly scolded him. At one point I asked, "Don't you know how sacred those moments are?" Sheepishly he answered, "I do now."

We struggle to do what is best for those we teach, and this is not always to their liking. It may not make us popular, but we are not there to be popular. Teachers, like parents, sometimes have to practice tough love. This is painful. Despite personal suffering, we need to stick to principles and teach with a tender tenacity. Jesus wasn't always popular either.

Our task is to use discipline as a tool to form students who know the value of discipline. Someday they may echo the words of actress Julie Andrews: "Some people regard discipline as a chore. For me, it is a kind of order that sets me free to fly."

For Your Reflection

- How would you rate your classroom discipline?
- What has self-discipline helped you to do on a personal level?
- What particular characteristics of those you teach make discipline a challenge?

CHAPTER
one

ℰᴁ **D**eveloping Positive Attitudes

Identifying Potential Problems

Starting Off Right

Creating Your Own Techniques

Instilling Mutual Respect

Presenting Fascinating Lessons

Leaning on Others

Involving the Students

Noticing Absolutely Everything

Emphasizing the Positive

THE CHILDREN'S STORY *The Little Engine That Could* conveys a valuable message for life. In case you have forgotten, the little engine conquers a large hill by repeating, "I think I can, I think I can." If we think we can, we can. Our mental outlook to a great extent determines our success or failure. To give an example, if we are walking across a beam and think we will fall, in all likelihood we will. Also, more and more evidence indicates that our physical health is largely a matter of mind. It follows then that positive attitudes towards ourselves and those we teach will yield positive effects. Visualize yourself as a vital and successful teacher, and chances are that is exactly what you will be.

Cultivate a healthy self-concept

The Church and in particular the parents of those you teach depend on you to educate young Christians. As a Catholic school teacher or a catechist, you have something very precious to hand on, over and above the content of secular subjects. You are cultivating a faith that will give meaning and joy to your students' lives now on Earth, and that affects their eternal well-being. Furthermore, what you teach them can make a difference in the universal Church and in the world.

You can accomplish this significant task if you have good discipline. To have good discipline you need a healthy self-concept.

Only then will you be strong enough to exercise leadership in your class.

When your self-esteem is at a low, consider these truths:

- As a teacher you have a special commission. God has chosen and called you to this ministry. As you try your best to fill this role, God will not fail you.

- You are a good person. Not everyone is willing to teach in a Catholic school when other schools (and professions!) offer larger salaries. And selfless are the catechists willing to devote time and energy to teach religion at a parish school for a minimal sum or nothing at all.

- You sacrifice television programs, games, and other enjoyable events in order to obtain and maintain certification, plan lessons, teach classes, and correct papers. You devote yourself to your students when you could be with family or friends.

- You deserve gratitude and respect.

Saint Paul wrote, "God has appointed in the church first apostles, second prophets, third, teachers; then deeds of power, then gifts of healing, forms of assistance, forms of leadership, various kinds of tongues" (1 Corinthians 12:28). Notice that in his list teachers supersede miracle workers!

Give yourself reminders

During difficult periods you might echo the Little Engine and keep muttering to yourself, "I think I can have good discipline." It may be more effective to write one of the following reminders in your manual or at the top of your lesson plan. You might place a copy of the list at home on your mirror or refrigerator where you will see it.

1. I am the teacher. They are just kids.
2. I am in the strategic position to guide the direction of the class.
3. I am older, wiser, more experienced, (and maybe larger) than my students.
4. I have been chosen for this ministry.
5. I am loved by God and deserve respect.
6. I am a professional.

As you teach, your whole being should declare that you have a good self-concept: your posture, the way you walk, your voice, and your gestures. Everything about you ought to radiate confidence. Teachers who convey timidity and insecurity invite students to take advantage of them. Children need strong role models. In a classroom they need a forceful, stouthearted person to take charge.

Sometimes students' behavior erodes our good self-concept. We begin to think there's something wrong with us. Believing we're failures, we become depressed. We dread walking into the classroom. In this situation it helps to talk to someone and even invite an observer to our class to offer an objective perspective and advice.

Decide your role

How you see yourself determines your teaching style, the atmosphere of the classroom, and ultimately your students' behavior. Here are some possible self-images. Decide which, if any, fit you. Check the ones that do. Are they good or bad images?

_____ co-seeker of truth

_____ facilitator

_____ professional teacher

_____ guide at the side

_____ sage on the stage

_____ witness

_____ committed Christian

_____ minister

_____ salesperson

_____ police officer

_____ military general

_____ pal

_____ entertainer

If you are convinced that you are teaching in Jesus' name and with the Holy Spirit as an invisible helper, what kind of teacher will you be?

Always be a model

Students need models more than critics. They require people who show what it's like to be made in God's image and likeness, to be redeemed by Christ, and to be a temple of the Holy Spirit. Therefore they ought to see in you a wholesome pride, hope, courage, and joy. To adapt Pope Paul VI's famous statement: "Modern children listen more willingly to witnesses than to teachers, and if they do listen to teachers, it is because they are witnesses." Aim for self-improvement. Know yourself and strive to reflect these Christian virtues:

Patience . . . to respond calmly to the student who asks in every class, "Why do we have to learn this stuff?"

Understanding . . . to separate the behavior from the child

Integrity . . . to refrain from speaking about a student's faults in front of others

Perseverance . . . to try again after a lesson fails

Knowledge . . . to answer questions or at least know where to find the answers

Discipline . . . to teach a good lesson no matter how you feel

Love . . . to cherish your students.

Along with an aura of authority, radiate enthusiasm, joy, and calm. This will help children respect and like you at the same time. When you do not feel enthusiastic, joyful or calm, rely on the act-as-if principle. Acting as if we feel or behave a certain way helps make the feeling or behavior a reality.

Have a high opinion of your students

In education courses a favorite story is that of a teacher whose roster contained what she thought were IQ scores. During the year the students she assumed were very intelligent did remarkably better than the rest. Then she discovered that the IQ scores were actually locker numbers!

Students tend to live up to a teacher's expectations. If you like the children you teach and convey to them that you think they are great, they probably won't disappoint you. Show that you have confidence in them and make them feel that you care about them.

Don't allow negative attitudes of other teachers to color your attitude toward a child or class. Let each year be a new opportunity for the children.

Refrain from unfavorably comparing your present class to classes you had in the past or to other classes. This is especially dangerous if you do this aloud in the presence of the children themselves.

If you are teaching the same grade you taught the previous year, remember that when the students left you at the end of the year, they were older and therefore more mature than the new students you face now.

Get to know your students as individuals

Cultivate a good relationship with your children. If your students sense that you dislike them, anything you do will be perceived negatively. Here are ways to learn about the children you teach . . . and let them learn about you:

- Arrive early to class so you can chat with your students. (They will also realize how important the class is to you if you are early.)
- Show interest in them by asking questions.
- On the first day of class have your students fill in a personal questionnaire to inform you of their siblings, favorite TV show, hobbies, a unique thing about themselves, and what they think about Jesus, history, math, or whatever you will be teaching that year.
- Invite their suggestions.
- In discussions draw their experiences from them.
- Ask the students for their opinions and feelings.
- At the end of class, stay in the room a while in order to be available to talk with students.

Assume that your students are good and that they really want to grow in knowledge of the world and their faith. Realize that they are not angels, but neither were you when you were their age.

Be aware that discipline problems are usually caused by needs that aren't being met, such as the need for security or affection. Many infractions are, in reality, defense mechanisms. Children who think they are inadequate or unworthy act in unsociable and self-defeating ways. Sometimes they will act impulsively without thinking—just as we sometimes do. Never give up on them. Do your utmost to counsel them and challenge them to be their better selves.

Love your problem children

Usually there is at least one child we wish would disappear. The problem child is a challenge to us to be Christ-like. Approach this student as a child of God and someone in whom God is living. Reject the behavior, not the person and never show dislike for the student. Pray for an honest love of him or her. Keep in mind the Master Teacher who goes after the lost sheep and of whom it was said, "He will not break a bruised reed or quench a smoldering wick" (Matthew 12:20). Be prepared to give a second chance, and a third, and a fourth. . . . The student who is the most difficult is the one who most needs your love and compassion.

During my first year of teaching religion to ninth graders, I felt like a dismal failure. The students were smart and constantly challenged what I did and said. They seemed to have little respect for me. In particular, I could count on one bright girl named Barbara to throw a monkey wrench into my well-planned lessons. Near the end of the year while correcting tests, I discovered this note Barbara had added to her essay: "Sister, you probably won't believe this, but I go to daily Mass and Communion. Something you said a while ago made me realize how important my faith is."

Not all teachers have a Barbara to reassure them that they do make a difference. Some of us will have to wait for such gratification until the end of time! I imagine many of us will meet our most troublesome students in the heavenly realm and blurt out, "What are you doing here?" It is only then that we'll hear the answer: "Something you said a while ago made me realize how important my faith is."

Difficult students can be like the irritating particle of dust in an oyster that eventually becomes a pearl. Be patient and kind, and the results may surprise you.

If a child has a serious problem, however, get outside help. Professional help may be needed. You might explore alternative methods of education like tutoring, instruction by parents, or transferring the student to another class. Your steps may be the best for the child and also prevent him or her from jeopardizing the learning of the rest of the class.

Keep in mind Rabbi Abraham Heschel's observation: "Care is half the cure."

Aim for a comfortable order

Not every teacher recognizes healthy classroom discipline. It is a comfortable order that frees students to learn efficiently. Comfort and order must be in a delicate balance. When either one is overstressed, discipline deteriorates. Two examples of the extremes illustrate this point.

1. Miss Lee sets out to make her hour-long religion class a pleasant experience. She tries to be a pal to her students. She ignores a lot of misbehavior such as talking out because she doesn't want to offend anyone. She lets the students eat

in class and have extra free time in order to win their favor. Soon the children aren't listening to her and learning is blocked. Miss Lee had made things too comfortable. In the end, no one is comfortable, least of all Miss Lee.

2. On the other hand, Mr. Hanson desires to run a tight ship. He seldom smiles or tries anything new for fear his seventh graders will get out of hand. Slight infractions are dealt with harshly. Soon children are tense and afraid to exercise initiative or even to ask questions. Learning is blocked. Mr. Hanson's emphasis on order has converted his students into scared robots instead of Christians who are "an alleluia from head to toe."

Somewhere between these two extremes of anarchy and dictatorship lies a well-disciplined classroom of controlled freedom. Once the teacher recognizes what it is, he or she can pursue it by two means:

1. Eliminating distractions, external or psychological, that hamper learning,

2. Presenting lessons in such a meaningful and enticing way that students want to do what they ought to do.

Some natural-born teachers achieve a comfortable order automatically. Others of us have to work at it. The quest for good discipline demands self-discipline, not only from the children but from us as well.

People alive with faith and the joy it brings have the greatest impact on others. You do not have to be a sourpuss or an ogre to establish a well-ordered class. Rather, it is the teacher who teaches with zest, love, and a dash of humor who elicits the most cooperation from students. In particular, religion teachers must remember that they are delivering the Good News, not the Bad News!

In addition to faith and joy, the following traits won't hurt either:

Be professional!
Be businesslike and efficient as you teach. Your style should clearly reflect that class time is important to you.

Be confident!
Try to appear confident and sure of yourself, even when you are not. Doubtfulness and indecisiveness are detected by children and soon give rise to problems.

Be dressed suitably!
Wearing something better than what you wear around the house shows respect for your students, your subject, and your role.

Be a teacher!
Remember that your job is to teach, not to tell combat stories or deliver monologues on how you succeeded in business or raised a family.

Be dignified!
Don't interpret or react to discipline infractions personally. Maintain your poise even though you may be seething inside. Avoid words and actions that are beneath your dignity as a teacher.

Be firm and gentle!
Strive to master the art of combining firmness and gentleness, of correcting without crushing, and of stimulating without discouraging.

For Your Reflection

- How do you feel about your ministry as a teacher in a Catholic school or a parish school of religion?

- Are you satisfied with the images you checked in the list on pages 4-5? What would you like to see yourself as?

- What virtue(s) of a successful teacher do you need to strengthen?

CHAPTER
two

Developing Positive Attitudes

Identifying Potential Problems

Starting Off Right

Creating Your Own Techniques

Instilling Mutual Respect

Presenting Fascinating Lessons

Leaning on Others

Involving the Students

Noticing Absolutely Everything

Emphasizing the Positive

Before a stage performance, to insure a smooth program the director oversees each detail. Lines are rehearsed, costumes and props are checked and put in place, lighting and sound systems are adjusted, and stand-ins are at hand. While preparing for class, teachers need to be as careful and conscientious as directors in spotting problems and averting tragedies. An ounce of prevention is worth a pound of cure. It is said that ninety percent of discipline problems are preventable. That leaves only ten percent for us to handle!

A statement in the *General Catechetical Directory* holds true for all teachers: "The basic concern of the catechist is to choose and create suitable conditions that are necessary for the Christian message to be sought, accepted, and more profoundly investigated" (71). So, don't ignore serious problems, even when dealing with them makes you uncomfortable. You are responsible for seeing that your students learn.

Check every aspect of the class

Your Teaching Space
A well-prepared environment can forestall discipline problems. Students find it easier to learn in a clean, neat, organized room— one that is large enough so they aren't crowded, but small enough that they aren't lost in it either.

If possible, decorate the room in the soothing colors of green, blue, and purple rather than the exciting colors of yellow, orange, and red. Be sure there is good lighting either above or behind the students. See that bright sun isn't blinding them or creating a glare. If the room is too hot or too cold, adjust the thermostat. There should be sufficient ventilation as well. When the room gets stuffy, open a window.

Above all, be sure that your teaching space is quiet, conducive to learning. If you are teaching religion, your classroom should be a special sacred space for speaking about God and praying. Children should be able to tell that religion is not just another class. Arrange the room to be attractive, warm, and inviting, and create a congenial, religious atmosphere in the following ways.

- Set up a prayer corner with an attractive cloth, a Bible, flowers, candles, incense, and religious images.
- Display inspiring posters.
- Create a religion bulletin board.
- Add a live plant or two.
- Play inspirational music before class and during quiet work times.
- Close the door and pull shades or close blinds to insulate the children from distractions.

Your assigned teaching space may have an unfavorable environment. Do what you can to solve the problems. Here are some typical problems and possible solutions:

If you share a large room with other classes, seat your students so they can't watch them.

If the room has a distracting or tempting display, make a portable screen from a large packing carton and set it up to block the display. Such a "screen" can also be used to hang posters or student work related to the topics being studied.

If you have no blackboard or whiteboard, use a large writing pad and markers.

If you have no overhead or laptop projector, make a flannel board by covering a piece of cardboard with flannel. Cut out figures from heavy paper and glue a small piece of sandpaper behind them so that they will adhere to the flannel.

Furniture

Seats should be large enough so that the students aren't cramped and low enough so that their feet touch the floor. Tables should have room for knees. If you are a catechist in a parish school of religion and the desks or chairs are not suitable, have children sit on carpet pieces or pillows.

A semicircular arrangement of desks is preferable to rows. It is more conducive to discussion and enables you to supervise children more easily and make eye contact with them. Furniture should be arranged so that traffic is no problem. Keep the desks free from doodling. Remove graffiti immediately because it tends to multiply.

Equipment

Equipment can be a boon or a bane. When working properly, it is a wonderful teacher assistant. Have all equipment set up, tested, and ready to run before class begins. Avoid tragedies like beginning to play a DVD on Moses and seeing Paul Bunyan appear, or needing to hunt for a CD player that works after you have the students quieted and ready to listen to a song. If setting up equipment wastes class time or if it is not properly adjusted, students will make their own entertainment.

Here are some practical tips about equipment.

- Have bulb replacements close at hand and know how to change them.

- Make sure that everyone can see the screen or board.

- Keep the board clean and supplied with chalk. If a piece of chalk squeaks, break it in half.

- Use colored chalk or markers for emphasis and interest.

- When depending on equipment that requires batteries or electricity, have a back-up plan in case of power failure.

- Practice using the computer and projector to insure that they work and that you know how they work.

- See that all electrical cords will not be run into or tripped over.

- Return all materials to the proper place so you can find them the next time you need them.

Class Size

Too many students in a class may cause problems. Large classes can be divided and taught by different teachers or on different days. If this isn't possible, ask for a teacher's aide or a parent to assist you. An extra person can keep an eye on your class when your back is turned, as well as take attendance, hear prayers in religion class, and check homework.

Team teaching may be a possibility. Combining two classes frees one person for supervision and management tasks.

The previous year's teacher is a good resource for advice in dealing with your students, especially if the group is large. Remember, though, that children change. Moreover, the way they related to another teacher may not be the way they relate to you.

Your Schedule

If class meets at a time or on a day that is problematic, try to change it. If a school schedule presents a problem, adapt it. Once I taught in a religion program that scheduled a fifteen-minute recess in the middle of class. The time usually expanded, and the particularly rowdy children often got into trouble. I cancelled the recess for my students, but in exchange let them put on a play in each class, which they loved to do.

Lesson Content

When those you teach see the value in what they are being taught, discipline is inherently there. Point out why the topics you are teaching are important.

Preview material and any audiovisuals to spot anything (topics, pictures, scenes) that might cause your class to get restless or upset. Plan ahead how to present that potentially disruptive material. For example, at one elementary school all of the children were shown the movie *Brother Sun and Sister Moon* about Saint Francis of Assisi. It includes a realistic portrayal of Francis divesting himself of his clothes before the bishop. From the students' boisterous reactions, it would have been good if the teachers had prepared them for this scene.

Supplies and Materials

Keep supplies clean and in working order. Have a few extra supplies, handouts, and worksheets on hand in case you need more than you anticipated. Make your extra pencils and pens a distinctive color so you can tell when a student has borrowed one.

If you are a catechist in a parish school of religion, provide pencils or pens, crayons and markers, scissors and glue, and collect them after each class. If you teach in someone else's classroom, store your supplies in a box or a dishpan and bring them to class with you.

Going to Church

If you are planning a lesson in your parish church, or if you will be attending a special Mass with your class, prepare children ahead of time for what they will be doing. In church they tend to sit shoulder to shoulder like sardines, and this can lead to behavior problems. If possible, have them space themselves one to a kneeler or about a yard apart. During a Mass or prayer service, sit behind the students where you can see them. If your whole school is involved, arrange for older and younger students to sit together. Both groups will be better behaved. If parents attend, invite them to sit with their children.

Your Teaching Style

A history of noisy or unruly classes indicates that you may be doing something wrong. Know your weaknesses and decide how to remedy them or compensate for them. For example, you might talk too fast, too slowly, or too much. You might have an idiosyncrasy or mannerism that annoys the class. Perhaps you are cross or irritable, and you aren't even aware of it.

Sometimes the noise in the class is caused by the teacher who closes books with a bang, walks heavily, slams doors and drawers, teaches in a voice loud enough for everyone in the hall to hear, and uses yelling to discipline. Children tend to imitate this loud behavior, so make sure you don't have such noisy habits.

Aim to be not so much a sage on the stage as a guide at the side. This will keep you from dominating the lesson. By the way, you don't have to pretend to know everything. Admit when you need to do some research to answer a question, or, better yet, challenge the students to do the research. Also, when you make a mistake, admit it.

Remove temptations

When you notice students with playthings, rubber bands, notes, cell phones, electronic games, and the like, take the things away immediately, but promise to return them to the owners at the end of class.

Use proximity control. When you suspect a student is misbehaving or will misbehave, move near him or her.

When students are engaged in an independent activity, or when you are conferring privately with one student, situate yourself in the back of the class. Your presence behind the class will deter inappropriate acts because the students will think your attention is still on the whole class.

Make sure you can see the students' hands. If you are a catechist teaching in a room with desktops that open, turn the desks around so that the students can't reach into them.

Always have an activity planned to keep students busy from the first moment they walk in the door, even before the official beginning of class. Give them a worksheet, have them prepare passages to be read in class, or direct them to sign up on the board for parts in plays.

Make note of the students who get into trouble when they are near each other. Separate them and keep them separated.

Have meaningful options ready for those who finish an activity before the rest of the class.

Never leave any class unsupervised, no matter what the reason!

Be sensitive to students

Some teachers fail because they are good at the subject but bad at dealing with children. Therefore make a sincere effort to know the characteristics of the age level you are teaching: the children's developmental stage, their interests, and their hobbies.

Get to know your students personally and quickly. Learn their names and use them so that each student in your class feels important. Knowing names also gives you a better hold on the class. You might even memorize the roster before you meet the students. This makes it easier to connect the names with the faces.

Find out who requires special attention so they do not disrupt the class. Meet with the students' parents. Learn the home situations of problem students. Their misconduct may be due to having to deal with their parents' divorce, their brother's drug habit, the death of a beloved grandmother, or being abused. Be alert to students who have special needs because of disabilities. Learn from their parents or other teachers how to facilitate those children's learning. Identify students who have a hard time relating to the others.

As the children enter the room, greet them cheerfully, by name if possible. Pay attention to their conversations and moods. This will alert you to anything that may block their receptivity to your lesson and prepare you to cope with it.

Be sensitive to your students as individuals. Notice that David is down in the dumps and that Melissa has new glasses.

Some discipline problems are related to health. If you suspect that a child has a health-related problem, contact the parents and suggest that he or she have a physical examination.

Notice when students appear restless or bored during an activity and be flexible enough to change it. When young children are bored, they start fidgeting more than usual and act up. Older students doodle, talk, sigh, yawn, look around, or stare.

Never "project" that you are too busy to be bothered by the children in your class.

One teacher stands at the door and shakes each student's hand as a sign of peace as the class leaves.

For Your Reflection

- What aspects of your teaching situation are less than perfect? What can you do about them?

- How can you make your teaching space more attractive and welcoming?

- Which students in your class do you know least?

CHAPTER
three

Developing Positive Attitudes

Identifying Potential Problems

✍ **S**tarting Off Right

Creating Your Own Techniques

Instilling Mutual Respect

Presenting Fascinating Lessons

Leaning on Others

Involving the Students

Noticing Absolutely Everything

Emphasizing the Positive

Priscilla was not a good student, and I probably didn't teach her much. But one day during a detention period, she taught me an important lesson. She remarked, "You know, Sister, as soon as a teacher walks into a room, we know if she can handle us." Discipline is largely a matter of beginnings: our first lesson, our lessons in the blueprint stage, our readiness for the students, and our preparation of the environment and equipment.

Good classroom management begins with day one. That first class is as crucial as the premiere of a television series. Often it determines whether or not we will hold our audience.

You never get a second chance to make a good first impression, and what should it be? We want to appear businesslike but caring, efficient yet relaxed, knowledgeable but open to the students' ideas. We want to be someone the children can trust. Begin to build a good student-teacher rapport by your friendliness.

Always teach something in the first class. On the first day it's likely that you will have your students' attention more than in succeeding days. Take advantage of it. Move directly into the subject in order to let your class know you mean business.

Deal firmly and quickly with any incidents that arise on the first days, or you will lose credibility. It is almost impossible to restore order if you begin with a casual, lenient attitude.

Know where you are going

In Lewis Carroll's *Alice in Wonderland,* Alice conversed with the Cheshire Cat:

Alice asked, "Would you tell me, please, which way I ought to go from here?"

"That depends a great deal on where you want to get to," said the Cat.

"I don't much care where—" said Alice.

"Then it doesn't matter which way you go."

Unlike Alice, we teachers must have our destinations clearly in mind. As we lead our students on the year's journey, our goals are our guide. Before class begins, use your manual to decide what you want your students to know or do by the end of the year. Think big. A fifth-grade teacher might set this goal: I want my students to grow in appreciation of the Eucharist. A third-grade teacher might have as a goal that every student will be able to write a good paragraph. Formulate your goals in one or two statements.

Having a sense of direction will make you more determined and conscientious, and consequently, more successful.

Set the tone and expectations

Before the school year begins, send your students postcards welcoming them to your class. If you don't have your class list early enough to do this, prepare a handwritten note for each child, making each note slightly different. Distribute the notes the first day. This will set a nice tone to the class and initiate a good relationship between you and the children.

Share with the students your hopes and goals for the year. Stress the importance of the class. Convey high expectations for your students. To expect mediocrity is an insult. Tell your children that you expect them to bring their books to class, to come on time, and to participate in class. Insist that they do neat work. Keep your standards high all year. Expressing hopes and expectations acts as a self-fulfilling prophecy. "I know you'll show the younger children how to behave during Mass" works better than "Those of you who act up during Mass will be in big trouble!"

A traditional adage for teachers is "Don't smile before Christmas." Although we definitely should not take that advice literally, there is wisdom behind it. A teacher must be businesslike and not too friendly until class control is secured. The first few weeks are comparable to a honeymoon. During that time, students sometimes test the teacher. By Christmas the teacher should have firmly established discipline.

If students fail to meet up to your expectations, have them repeat the activity. For example, if they run to get in line, send them back to their seats and tell them to line up again but this time by walking, not running.

Try to create a classroom family. With the right guidance you and those you teach will form bonds that will be expressed in mutual concern and support.

Formulate realistic rules

Sometimes students will honestly not know what your idea of good classroom behavior is unless you spell it out. In one of my classes, several freshmen persisted in calling out answers. I discovered that at the school they previously attended their teacher encouraged this.

Declare the rules for your class and review the school rules. The students need to know their limits. If you don't define them, they will seek them by trial and error.

Give the reasons for the rules. Here are examples: There is quiet in the hall out of courtesy for other classes. In class there is no gum chewing because you don't like it and your wishes are to be respected, and more practically, because gum tends to end up on desk bottoms, the floor, and shoes.

Let children know you are concerned that they are safe and secure in the classroom. Explain that rules create a good climate for learning. Children actually appreciate reasonable rules; they know they are for their own protection and benefit. They also appreciate having the rules enforced. Students are really not happy if they can run all over the teacher and get away with it. Moreover, when one or a few students break the rules without censure, the rest of the class is frustrated and angry—and rightly so.

Inform the students of the consequences of not keeping the rules or at least have these clearly in your own mind. You might say, for example, "Students who text or tweet during class will have their cell phones confiscated." Penalties issued on the spur of the moment in the heat of anger could easily be disproportionate to the offense.

Allow democratic participation. Let those you teach share in the formulation of the rules as well as in determining the consequences of breaking them. This will give them ownership of the class. It will also somewhat relieve you of the job of being the enforcer because punishment will be the natural result of a transgression. In determining punishment for a specific incident, however, take into consideration the unique needs of individuals and the circumstances.

You might have children sign a contract accepting responsibility to abide by the classroom rules.

Send home or email a letter explaining school and classroom policies so that parents are informed about your class and can support you.

Post the class rules where everyone can see them.

Here are some rules about rules:

1. State the rules positively. For instance, instead of saying, "Do not chew gum," say "Throw any gum in the wastebasket before class." Rather than, "Do not mark up your books," say, "Show respect for your religion books. Keep them clean."

2. State the rules briefly so that they are more easily remembered. For example, "Be kind."

3. Make no more than five rules. Multiplying rules multiplies problems. A teacher I know had just one good rule: "Only one person speaks at a time." This meant that when the teacher or a student spoke, everyone else listened.

4. All rules should facilitate learning. If there is no good reason for a rule, don't make it.

Have a seating plan

Start out the year by making a seating plan that has the students in alphabetical order to help you remember their names. After you know the children's names and them, arrange their seats strategically. Seat someone who is habitually tardy near the door. Separate students who are like fire and dynamite when they are together. Seat children who have poor sight or hearing in the front. Also put troublemakers near you.

At some point later you may decide to let the students choose their own seats. Always be ready to change a seat if necessary. Keep an up-to-date seating plan for substitute teachers.

Establish routines

Introduce routines and put them into practice immediately to prevent wasted time and needless frustration later. In advance decide the most efficient way to accomplish routine tasks. Assure children that classroom policies are not written in stone. Exceptions may be made when necessary. Routines that save time and create order in a classroom include the following:

Beginning class

As the students walk into class, you might have classical music playing quietly to settle them and to set a businesslike tone. Begin promptly; don't wait for stragglers. Many religion teachers and catechists like to begin with prayer. You might prefer to pray within a lesson and begin with a joke, a simple call to order, or twenty seconds of silence.

Clearing desks

Coats and jackets should be out of the way, on hooks or in lockers. Tell the students to put their books under the desk until they are needed. Their desks should be cleared of everything at the beginning of class so they are free to concentrate on the lesson.

Taking attendance

Call names and have the children respond "Here" or take attendance informally, scanning the class before the lesson begins. Catechists might teach the children to take attendance: Have their names on papers cut into shapes and spread the papers near the door. As the children enter the room, they find their name and place it in a box. Be creative in designing shapes for the attendance slips and the locations where to put them. For instance, children can pick up a flower slip and place it in a vase or "garden." You might designate an area on the bulletin board "Out" and "In." Tack the slips under *Out*. When the students arrive, they move their names to the *In* spot.

Raising hands to answer

The practice of raising hands allows one student to answer at a time so that the response is heard and understood. Avoid repeating a student's answer, which discourages children from listening to one another. Encourage them to speak loudly enough for everyone to hear.

Distributing and collecting papers and supplies

The way you distribute and collect papers and supplies will depend on the size of your class and the seating arrangement. The important thing is to make your chosen procedure a habit. Papers and supplies can be distributed by the first person in each row and collected by the last person.

To save time, you might have the children pick up papers and supplies as they enter the room. Similarly, instead of collecting these materials, have children deposit them in an assigned place as they leave the room.

If your class is in rows, have the papers passed up from the back to the front. Then have the student in the first seat of the first row collect them across the front and place them on your desk. You may wish to have the students bring up their papers individually to give them a little exercise after a quiet activity.

To prevent squabbles, remind children always to write their names on papers and art projects.

Distributing and collecting books

Appoint a student in each row or group to distribute and collect books, or see that they are on the desks ahead of time. If children have their own books or Bibles, make sure their names are on them the first day to avoid mix-ups.

Sharpening pencils

It's best to have children sharpen pencils before class. Have extra pencils on hand to replace those that break during the lesson. Direct children to leave on your desk a personal belonging in place of the borrowed pencil as a reminder to return it.

Going to the restroom

Children should take care of going to the restroom before class. Allow for emergencies, however. You'll find that if students ask to go to the lavatory or to get a drink of water during class and you know it's not a pressing need, if you ask "Can you wait?" they usually respond "Yes" and return to their seats.

Moving from place to place as a group

Establish stopping places for the leader so that any stray students can merge again with the group. Bring up the end of the line yourself.

Forming groups

Assign the students to groups for discussions and projects. Be prepared to change the groups during the year. Let different students experience being a group leader.

Straightening up the room after class

Make children responsible for cleaning up their own territory. Appoint helpers to collect scraps in the wastebasket, erase and wash the board, and do other housework tasks.

Assigning jobs

Choose children for various jobs. The more students you can involve, the better. They can close the door at the beginning of class, take the attendance slip to the office, answer the door, distribute papers, water the plants, and operate equipment.

Especially give jobs to hyperactive students, shy students, and students who crave attention. Use these jobs as privileges that can be given or taken away as a means of discipline.

Develop positive relationships

Don't just teach a class, teach children! Get to know them on a one-to-one basis and develop a good relationship. You might be the only friend some children have. They will not be likely to do anything to spoil that relationship.

Express sympathy to your students in times of illness or misfortune. Call, send a card, or visit them. Also, let the children get to know you. Be willing to share yourself with the class. If you play the guitar, use it in a lesson. If you are artistic (and even if you're not), make souvenir cards for your students for Christmas or as prizes or surprise gifts.

When you put time and effort into starting off on the right foot, the rest of the year will go more smoothly for you and your students.

For Your Reflection

- What rules in your classroom are your students aware of? What input have they given to these rules?

- What routines need to be set in your class? Where will you start first?

- Are you usually consistent with your routines? If not, why not? How do the children react to them?

CHAPTER
four

Developing Positive Attitudes

Identifying Potential Problems

Starting Off Right

Creating Your Own Techniques

Instilling Mutual Respect

Presenting Fascinating Lessons

Leaning on Others

Involving the Students

Noticing Absolutely Everything

Emphasizing the Positive

THE FIFTH-GRADE TEACHER where I once taught was having difficulty with an exuberant redhead named Jim. In desperation, she taped a green scapular under his desk, hoping that the Blessed Virgin Mary would help her. The scapular remained until one day when for a lesson the teacher hid objects around the room and told the class to find them. Jim discovered the scapular under his desk, assumed it was one of these objects, and claimed it as a prize. Whether or not the scapular affected his behavior in class is unknown. The last I heard of him, he was running for a government office!

Unless you diligently employ tactics for good discipline from September to June, even a class that begins like a dream can deteriorate into a nightmare. You do not have to be domineering and overbearing to have good discipline—a master instead of a minister. A master forces students to behave; a minister guides and encourages them.

Each teacher has to develop techniques that are right for him or her. These come naturally or are learned from other teachers. Of course, the ideal strategy is to make yourself so well liked that the children wouldn't think of displeasing you!

The following are some ways to survive now that classes are no longer taught "to the tune of a hickory stick." Always begin with the gentlest form of discipline. Then if that fails, resort to a stronger method. Keep in mind that your most drastic measure soon becomes the standard.

Use nonverbal signals

Most of us have a repertoire of nonverbal signals. These enable us to get a point across without disturbing the class and interrupting the lesson. Among the no-fuss ways to quell misbehavior is the classic stern look. Other teacher looks (which you can practice in front of a mirror) are warning, dismay, disapproval, anger, amazement, and shock. A raised eyebrow, a hard stare, a certain smile, a waving finger, and a mere shake of the head are also effective.

Send silent messages by means of gestures. Glance at an offender and point to the chart of rules. Develop codes like the following.

- Pointing to the wastebasket: "Throw out the gum."
- Pointing to the floor and making an upward sweep with the hand: "Pick up the paper."
- Putting your finger over your lips: "Quiet."
- A thumbs-up: "That's good."
- Drawing a finger across your neck: "Watch it!"

If a student is not working at an assigned task, quietly go to him or her and touch the textbook or worksheet. Often this is all that is needed. A friendly hand on the shoulder or gentle touch on the arm will also prompt students to get down to business.

Write a misbehaving student's name or initials on the board. This will usually stop the disruptive behavior. It will also remind you to speak to the child later.

Children will appreciate your tact in disciplining. Someone defined such tact as "raising your eyebrow instead of the roof."

To restore order in the midst of chaos, one teacher stood on her desk and immediately got everyone's attention. A dramatic move like this should be used sparingly because it soon loses its shock value.

Change your voice

To alert misbehaving students that you are aware of the mischief going on, change your voice as you are teaching. Slow down, increase the volume, lower the tone, speak very deliberately, or insert a meaningful pause. Do not, however, shout or raise the pitch of your voice. In fact, little children respond well to a whisper.

Reprimand privately

Often it is better to reprimand privately. This does not distract children who are working. It also prevents the guilty party from being a martyr in the eyes of the class.

Suppose you see a child making an airplane out of your carefully prepared worksheet. Go to the culprit's desk and whisper questions like these:

"Are you learning?"

"Is what you're doing helping the others to learn?"

"What are you doing?

"What should you be doing?"

"Can you do it?"

"Will you do it now?"

Keep children on task by making statements that are motivational rechargers. If you see a child daydreaming, for example, instead of working on an exercise in the textbook, whisper, "The sooner you finish, the more time you'll have for yourself."

Sometimes you can catch a student's eye when he or she is about to throw a spitball or pass a note and just say "Un-uh," or an emphatic "No!"

If you speak to a child privately in front of the room, position yourself so the offender's back is to the class and you can still keep an eye on the other children.

Cultivate a sense of humor

Children like teachers who can tell a joke and take a joke. Spice your lessons with a bit of humor now and then, and laugh with children when something humorous happens. Be able to laugh at yourself. It makes you more human and approachable.

Most of us dislike being told what to do. Orders can make us angry or feel degraded. Students will respond to reminders positively if they are delivered with a dose of humor. To hurry her class along when they are moving to church, a teacher friend of mine says, "My grandmother walks faster than you." When it looks as though someone is cheating by looking at someone else's paper, I comment, "This is not the time to do eye exercises." The students get the point.

Sometimes you might be able to kid students out of ill humor or away from misbehavior. When a guest speaker was about to address my twelfth graders, I was concerned about the class clown and the thorn in my side. Bob was over six feet tall and large. (One day during homeroom period he fit a whole apple in his mouth!) By contrast I was a size 8 petite. Right before the speaker was to arrive, I walked over to Bob and whispered, "If you make one comment out of line, I will break every bone in your body." This ridiculous, unorthodox remark shocked him into silence. By the way, Bob became a high school history teacher and coach.

Plan a signal for getting attention

When you want the class's attention, simply say "If I could have your attention please," or use a signal like clapping your hands, ringing a bell, striking a chime, tilting a rain stick, playing a chord or a little tune on the piano, flicking the lights off and on, or whispering. A certain teacher puts her hands behind her head. One by one the children imitate her until everyone is ready. An alternative is to state, "Hands on top," putting your hands on top of your head; and the children respond, "We stop," putting their hands on top of their head.

Another technique is to make a certain word a signal to quiet down. This could be a silly word like *bamboozle* or *zip-a-dee-doo-dah* or a term related to a school subject like *denominator, haiku,* or *Columbus.* As a transition to settle the children after an activity, one teacher begins counting to ten in Spanish and all the children join in.

You might pronounce a word or phrase to which children respond. Here are a few possibilities:

You	Children
Hocus pocus.	Now we focus.
Macaroni and cheese.	We freeze.
1, 2, 3, eyes on me.	1, 2, eyes on you.

An alternative is to clap a rhythm and the children respond by clapping a rhythm.

Warn children before it is time to conclude an activity so they have the satisfaction of completing it. Announce, "You have three more minutes" or "Start putting on the finishing touches."

Give and take "time out"

Little children who need time out because of misbehavior can be invited to cool down at a special table, on a designated chair, or on a throw rug. Older children, too, can benefit from being set apart from the group for a while to think things through. But do not send students out to the hall alone. They might disappear!

At times your entire class can become unruly. When this happens, stop teaching. Firmly state, "I'm waiting." If this has no effect, walk over to your desk and be seated. Pretend to be engrossed in correcting papers, looking over the manual, or some other task. Eventually the students will realize that you refuse to teach over their noise. Gradually they will settle down and look at you. Once there is silence, look up and ask, "How many are ready to learn something?" Undoubtedly every student's hand will be raised.

Use awards

"Bribery" works on all grade levels. For instance, agree to do something the children enjoy if there is one hundred percent cooperation during a difficult lesson. Peer pressure will come into play here—for the good.

Entice the students with creative promises. To persuade eight-year-old Kevin to eat his baloney sandwich, I told him that if he did, I would Indian wrestle with him. After lunch we went behind a screen in the office and had our match. I lost—but only because the principal was peering over the screen and making me laugh. For the rest of the year, this shared "secret" made Kevin and me friends.

Row races are popular with younger children. Assign each row a number and write the numbers in a column on the board or on a chart. Periodically add a star after the number of a row for such things as sitting tall, being ready to listen, trying to answer, working hard, or being quiet. At the end of the class or the week, give the winning row small prizes.

Remember that extrinsic motivation is not as powerful or as lasting as intrinsic motivation. Try to spur your children on to be good students for the sake of the sheer satisfaction, enjoyment, or challenge of it. Rewards and punishments may work momentarily but then have no significant influence on the children's lives. Our goal is not merely to control behavior during the time the children are in our class, but to form enduring habits, attitudes, and convictions.

Talk with the class

Communication is one of the most effective means to prevent, as well as to solve, problems in offices, in homes, and in classrooms. Now and then take time to talk with your class apart from the lessons. When you openly discuss what is underlying classroom happenings, you will be building rapport and creating a feeling of community.

If those you teach are affected by something that just occurred, talk about it for a while—a short while. For example, if they have just witnessed a car accident or the first snowfall, don't ignore these experiences but comment on them. The children's minds will be centered on them anyway. Sometimes unexpected events are "teachable moments," opportunities to teach lessons that will last a lifetime.

In particular, after some misfortune has resulted from misbehavior, discuss the incident with the students to make it a learning experience.

Give the class a pep talk on behavior whenever you sense they need one. Motivate the children to learn. Review the reasons for rules and urge the students to be mature and smart. Assure them of your care and support.

Call misbehavers by name

When reprimanding out loud, use a student's name. Be brief in your rebuke. A public scolding has a ripple effect. Other children will then avoid the misbehavior.

Sometimes it is sufficient merely to state what the student is doing wrong in order to change behavior: "Carol, you're talking."

In calling attention to a misdeed, make the problem the child's not yours. Ask, "What did you do? What are you going to do about it?" However, do not ask, "Why did you do this?" The child probably doesn't know.

Avoid reprimanding an individual repeatedly or at length during class. A curt "That's enough!" may put an end to the undesirable behavior.

To recapture the attention of students who are talking or daydreaming, call on them. (Note that children who have Attention-Deficit/Hyperactivity Disorder [ADHD] can be looking out the window but hear everything you say. Ask a question and they will prove it.)

Change a child's seat during a lesson if necessary

Divert a child who is misbehaving with a question. If Andy is poking the student in front of him, ask, "Andy, what part of the assignment did you find hardest?" or "Andy, would you please erase the board for us?"

Use a student's misbehavior to your advantage in a clever way to reinforce what you are teaching, surprise the class, and add new vitality to the lesson. For instance, suppose as you are talking about sharing our goods with others, Tommy is playing with a calculator he brought to class. Walk up to him, saying, "Christians are willing to share, just as I know Tommy is willing to give me this calculator for a little while. Tommy, I need your calculator. May I please borrow it?" Accept the calculator from Tommy and take it to your desk.

Be creative in giving positive orders

Commands express power, and power may evoke hostility or fear in children. Therefore, when you issue orders, disguise them. Here are two examples: Instead of saying, "Turn to page 64" state, "The story is on page 64." Instead of commanding, "Write a paragraph" say, "You will write a paragraph."

Likewise state warnings and reprimands positively. For instance, instead of declaring, "You're getting too noisy. Quiet down," say, "This writing activity needs concentration. Let's not talk during it."

Use the cooperative approach in giving an order: "*We'll* need to do this." "*We* need to move quickly and quietly."

Sometimes say thank you before the action is performed to elicit cooperation: "Thank you for getting into line quietly."

When children are not doing something they should be, ask them to do it rather than ordering them: "Would you please pick up that paper?" not "Pick up that paper."

Beware of giving directions that assume the children are working for you and not themselves. Avoid giving orders with "I want you to," "I need," or "I'd like you to."

Soften an order by pointing out when or where the children can do what they want. "Julie and Dawn, you can finish your conversation in ten minutes when class is over." "Bob, you can play that game at home, but not in this room."

What about incorrigible children? Give them papers on which to record each time you must correct them. This will help them realize how often they disrupt the class. It will also serve as a means of tracking progress.

Have private talks with misbehavers

The most effective way to deal with a misbehaving student is to talk with him or her privately. This personal approach is less embarrassing for the student and more honest because the child will not be performing in front of his or her peers. It also saves precious class time. Furthermore, devoting extra time to a student sends the signal that you really care. At the end of private talks, children should feel good about themselves and you.

Plan your talks to be positive and to reflect that you care for the student. Disarm with your opening statement instead of beginning with an attack. Say something like, "I'm concerned that something is bothering you" or "This isn't like you. What's wrong?"

First, make the guilty party aware of the problem unless he or she obviously knows what is wrong. Be firm and make it clear that you will not allow certain behavior in class. Explain that you have a responsibility to the whole class and to the students' parents that learning is taking place.

Second, lead the offender to reflect on how his or her behavior is affecting others and suggest how to make up for any wrongdoing. Guide the child to realize that the wrongdoing has actually hurt himself or herself.

Third, get the student to accept responsibility for his or her behavior and cooperatively determine how to eliminate the undesirable behavior, spelling out actions and consequences. Motivate the child to take steps to change by asking, "Do we have to make a big deal out of this or can we handle it ourselves?" Before the next class it is a good idea to remind the student of the plan mutually agreed upon for his or her improvement.

Forced apologies are rarely effective because they are probably insincere. If a child has hurt another child or the whole class, suggest an apology, but don't encourage hypocrisy. Besides, such an apology may lead the child to think that merely saying those words make up for any wrongdoing.

Guidelines for a conference

Throughout a student conference, try the following:

- Ask questions and listen to the child; really listen. These five questions would be appropriate:

    –What if everyone in the class did what you did?

    –What would your classmates say about what you did?

–How are things going with you?

–How is your behavior affecting others?

–What can I do to help you?

- Handle the child with gentleness and acceptance.
- Look into the child's eyes as you speak.
- Smile once in a while to convey acceptance.
- Make supportive statements like "I don't want the class to think badly of you" or "Let's see what we can do to lick this problem."
- Appeal to the child's desire to be mature and well liked.
- Plant seeds for further thought with brief comments like "If I were you, I wouldn't want to hurt my future" or "Do you really think this is true?"
- Strive to preserve a good relationship so that learning is not blocked in the future.

Move around the room

While children are working independently or in small groups, circulate, not only to supervise but to answer questions and to be of assistance. Avoid spending most of the time with just one group.

Some mischief is the result of students not being able to accomplish a task. Their frustration is expressed in the form of inappropriate behavior. When a child is not working, ask, "Are you having trouble?" or "Is this too hard for you?"

When necessary, a pat on the head, a hand on the shoulder, or a quick hug goes a long way in reassuring children that you care about them and that they count. (Be cautious and prudent in making any kind of physical contact with the students.)

Physical restraint might occasionally be necessary to keep children from harm. Be careful and speak soothingly to a child by saying things like "Take it easy. Everything will be all right. Just calm down."

Corporal punishment is not an option. Don't use it.

Have children write

Direct perpetrators to write reports about what happened. These reports provide a cooling-off period for the students and you. They can also assist in conferring with parents. During a conference with a child, discuss what was written.

As a form of punishment, have the children write essays about the pros and cons of their misbehavior. This will cause them to think about what they did and perhaps change their behavior.

Periodically solicit feedback from the students by passing out stationery and asking them to write you a letter about the class. They could tell you their feelings, make observations, ask questions, offer suggestions, or write anything else they would like to share with you. Assure them that what they write will be confidential unless you need someone's help to address a situation in the letter.

Put a suggestion box in your room so the children can have input. Sometimes their ideas and even their complaints will make us better teachers or lead to better lessons. You may find notes like "Go fly a kite" or worse, but offering students a chance to express their thoughts is worth it.

Pray often with children

The professor who taught calculus at the college I attended always began class with prayer. Sincerely pray with your students, not just formal prayers, but spontaneous prayer and centering prayer. Some teachers gather their children in a prayer circle with arms around one another and pray for intentions. Praying expresses and helps to create Christian community. The stronger your ties are with the students as a group, the better chance you have of being a formative influence on their behavior.

Do not feel guilty about giving children time for personal prayer in class. This might be the only time some of them pray.

Don't make God an enforcer

When reprimanding children, do not speak in such a way that they come to think of God as the all-seeing eye ready to zap them for any transgressions. God's reputation is easily ruined by such statements as "God is watching you" and "What would God say?"

Likewise lecturing, preaching, and moralizing during a time of correction do more harm than good. They evoke animosity, which leads to even more disorderly conduct. Instead, simply explain that you do not tolerate private conversations, slovenly work, and so forth. Challenge children to meet your expectations.

Furthermore, if you speak with a hesitant, timid, or pleading voice, you lose ground. When you are indecisive, vacillating, or look helpless, your authority weakens. Communicating rebukes in a firm, matter-of-fact way will get the best results.

For Your Reflection

- What are some techniques you remember from your experiences as a student? Do you use these now?

- What new techniques discussed in this chapter would you like to try in your class? What will you do first?

- In what ways do you talk about God with those you teach? Do you ever talk about God in the role of enforcer?

CHAPTER
five

Developing Positive Attitudes

Identifying Potential Problems

Starting Off Right

Creating Your Own Techniques

Instilling Mutual Respect

Presenting Fascinating Lessons

Leaning on Others

Involving the Students

Noticing Absolutely Everything

Emphasizing the Positive

IMAGINE THIS SCENARIO. A fifth-grade teacher is teaching about the greatest commandment. "Jesus told us to love another. Jerry, if you don't stop picking on Vicky, I'm going to start picking on you. . . . This is the second greatest commandment, that we love one another. Bob, who do you think you are that you can keep interrupting this class? And you, young lady, you wipe that smirk off your face. . . . Jesus said that the sign that we are Christians is that we love one another."

A class like this would make any lesson completely forgettable. A teacher should be a helpful, caring, competent, reliable, admirable person, someone the children could look up to and imitate. When we fail to act with respect, when we are rude, unreasonable, and unfair, we lose the students' respect. Even worse, they might mirror our behavior.

The way teachers treat us and speak to us stays with us for life. I can vividly recall my fifth-grade teacher's stinging remark when I wasn't able to answer a question in history class: "Glavich, you don't know beans from butter with the bag wide open." I never liked history much after that.

Realize that often it is not *what* you say but *how* you say it that makes the difference between respect and disrespect.

If our discipline methods are merely displays of power that intimidate children and render them powerless, how can we teach Jesus' message of having a heart for the poor and living the Beatitudes? Keep in mind the golden rule: "In everything do to others as you would have them do to you" (Matthew 7:12).

Following are some practical ways to model good behavior, teach in a truly Christian setting, and enjoy good discipline all year through.

Some don'ts for teachers

Shun verbal abuse. It undermines your authority rather than reinforces it. Above all, it alienates children. Don't nag, lose your temper, use sarcasm, humiliate or embarrass students, threaten, ridicule, insult children, call them names, or try to have the last word. You may be able to crush a troublemaker with one brilliant, withering remark, but consider what students learn when we resort to such methods to control them or to defend ourselves.

Avoid yelling. It is upsetting and casts a pall over the whole class. If you shout at the slightest provocation, either you will be ignored or you will unwittingly set up a game in which students delight in goading you to the exploding point. On the other hand, if you ordinarily speak calmly, when you do raise your voice a notch, children will be startled and listen.

Resist being drawn into futile disputes or arguments with a child. You may well be the loser in the class's opinion.

Never touch misbehaving students or grab an article from them. Such actions might unintentionally hurt them.

Avoid confrontation. The child might win. Try not to be placed on the defensive.

Don't dare children. They are likely to take you up on it, and then they will expect you to follow through.

Avoid using grades as a threat. That is never a good way to motivate children—especially in religion class.

Don't punish the whole class for the infraction of one child or a few. It is unjust to punish the innocent.

Avoid forced confessions. The accused student will probably lie. Simply state that you know what the child has done and you don't want it to happen again.

Don't use empty threats like, "If you don't finish that paper, you'll stay here all night." This kind of threat is dishonest and ineffective. Children know you don't mean it, and some of them see a threat as a challenge! Whenever you inform a student of a misbehavior's consequence, do carry it out.

Don't overact to minor infractions by delivering a grand tirade or worse. When a child is chewing gum after supposedly throwing it away, or when a student counters your directions with, "Why should I? It's a free country, isn't it?" you will probably see red. It might take the control of a saint not to shake the little monster until his or her teeth rattle. You are more apt to make an issue of a trivial matter when you are tired or in poor health.

Don't assign homework as a punishment. It may cause students to dislike the subject you are teaching. If it is religion, this would be especially unfortunate.

Don't interrupt a student who is speaking or answering a question.

Never belittle a child's answer. Not only will the child be embarrassed, but other students may be discouraged from answering. Manage to find something good to say about every sincere response.

Avoid making a scene in class for the sake of your ego, for instance, to protect your power.

Don't take out personal problems on your students. Leave your troubles outside the classroom. Be especially patient when you are having a down day. If you do lose control of yourself, an apology affords children the respect they deserve and teaches a powerful lesson.

Refrain from speaking about the faults of your students and their families unless you are honestly trying to help them. This is a matter of professional ethics.

Some do's for teachers

Always be polite. Use please, thank you, and you're welcome frequently when talking to your students. Common courtesy should be a ground rule in your classroom.

Respond to infractions quickly and fairly. Children understand and accept this kind of action.

Be consistent. Children need the security of knowing what to expect. If talking out warrants a reprimand one week, it deserves one the next week. If a humorous remark makes you laugh at the beginning of class, it shouldn't be the cause for detention at the end of class. If Tina is late and is punished, Tony, too, should be punished when he comes late. Mete out punishments objectively. To students, unfairness in a teacher is a mortal sin.

Make disciplinary actions constructive. Writing "I will not talk" a hundred times doesn't accomplish much except dirtying the board or wasting paper. Match the punishment to the crime if possible. For example, a student who writes on the desk should have to clean it and maybe the other desks in the room as well.

Focus on solutions. Suggest ways to make things right.

Discuss the action, not the personality. Correct, criticize, or condemn unacceptable behavior, not the children. This preserves their self-esteem. Say, "You have never finished an exercise on time" not "You are so lazy."

Give the students opportunities to save face. Offer alternatives. Children need to feel important and significant too. Sometimes you might have to back off. When a child says something disrespectful, delay reacting. Then ask, "I don't think I heard you correctly. What did you say?" Chances are that the child will retract the statement or apologize.

In confronting students, use "I-statements" rather than "you-statements." Beginning with you is accusing. Instead of saying, "You are disrupting the whole class by your comments," invite a response by saying, "I find it hard to teach when I'm constantly interrupted" or "I am angry because of what is going on." When children know the teacher is troubled by their behavior, they usually want to correct it.

End serious misbehavior promptly by saying, "Stop it," "That's enough," or "We don't do that." Recommend that the students quit before they get into more trouble. Then minimize rather than maximize the situation.

Keep individuals from jeopardizing the learning of others. Simply say, "Please see me after class" and move on. To put an end to a verbal battle, say, "We'll continue this conversation after class."

Use humor to keep your dignity and diffuse situations.

Convey affection for children even when reprimanding them. You might say, "I like you, but I don't like this behavior."

Let bygones be bygones. Forgiveness is the child's means to regain self-esteem after making a mistake.

Keep in mind that your goal is not to punish students but to facilitate discipline. You do not want to change just surface behavior, but basic attitudes.

For Your Reflection

- In what ways might you show more respect for those you teach?

- Is your method of dealing with discipline problems mature? Is it Christian?

- Can you think of examples of successful discipline techniques you have used? What are they?

CHAPTER
six

Developing Positive Attitudes

Identifying Potential Problems

Starting Off Right

Creating Your Own Techniques

Instilling Mutual Respect

Presenting Fascinating Lessons

Leaning on Others

Involving the Students

Noticing Absolutely Everything

Emphasizing the Positive

Most teachers and catechists agree that the strongest form of preventive discipline is good lessons. An engaging, solid lesson takes time to prepare. Very few people can successfully talk off the top of their heads while standing in front of a class. Children are quick to detect that the teacher is unprepared, and they proceed to carry out their own plans.

A well-planned lesson is usually interesting, taught with enthusiasm, and helps one to teach with confidence. Consequently, it holds children's attention, and they have neither the time nor the desire for disruptive behavior.

A teacher who cares plans care-fully!

Prepare well

Advance preparation is essential. All the good will in the world won't substitute for it. Imagine a surgeon going into an operating room without preparation, or a football team going onto the field without a strategy. We who are dealing with the minds and hearts and perhaps spiritual well-being of other human beings have an obligation to prepare.

Those educators who try to teach relying solely on the spontaneous inspiration of the Spirit, soon find their students following the lead of other spirits. Normally the Spirit works through us when we work. Preparation takes time and effort, discipline, and even sacrifice. But the rewards are worth it.

When we have created a sound plan and are familiar with it, our teaching flows smoothly with no awkward pauses and fumbling for pages. Students do not have time to get into mischief. If we are unprepared, while we are hemming and hawing and paging through the manual, not only is the clock ticking away, but Joey is gluing together the pages of someone else's book.

In addition, when we are prepared and have made the lesson our own, we are more confident and automatically convey this to the students. They sit up and take notice.

Ways to insure good lessons

Make the lessons long enough. Don't be caught with minutes to spare at the end of your lessons. Always plan more than you will need. Have an additional activity at hand to fill the time if necessary, perhaps a review game or a project.

Keep lessons unpredictable. Keep the students guessing. They should never know what to expect when they walk through the door for your class: games, independent work, art projects, discussion, group work, a video, or a guest speaker. Everyone likes novelty. More important, presenting material in various ways meets the needs of students who have different learning styles.

Keep them varied. Change activities in the course of a lesson. The younger the children, the more often change is needed. In general, children's attention span matches their age. According to this rule of thumb, a five-year-old has a five-minute attention span and a thirteen-year-old has a thirteen-minute attention span. For a change of pace, play a review game, teach a song, say a prayer, or move to a different location. The possibilities are endless.

How many ways can you think of for children to read a section in their textbooks or Bibles besides the usual "round robin" reading? Here are eight methods:

- Students read the section silently.
- You read it for them.
- They read it aloud together.
- They listen to a recording.
- One child reads the section aloud.
- Children read when called at random.
- Each child reads a paragraph—or a sentence!—going around the class in order.
- Students read aloud and at any point stop and call on a classmate to continue.

NOTE: Allow poor readers a chance to "pass" to spare them embarrassment.

Make lessons interesting. The material should hold the children's attention. A good lesson engages children's minds and hearts by relating to them, and it impels them to think and to respond. They usually find anything pertaining to their lives interesting. Make the effort to link what is being studied to their culture, needs, interests, and world if your manual doesn't do so. Show you students that the content has personal meaning for them. Religion more than any other subject offers opportunities for this.

Weave information from the daily news into your lessons. Bring in articles from newspapers and magazines and read parts of them to the class.

Take advantage of special days and seasons and work them into your lessons. Use purple paper during Lent. Give out Thanksgiving stickers during November. Tell the story of Saint Nicholas on his feast day.

Add personal stories and examples to your lessons to make them more interesting. However, don't overdo it!

Aim to have at least one activity in each lesson that the children will consider fun and exciting. This will help them look forward to your class.

Having a special visitor works wonders, too, especially if it is a parent. The novelty of a new person in the class charms some children away from misbehavior. It also motivates you to produce a better-than-usual lesson.

Make challenging lessons. Activities that are too difficult are frustrating, but those that are too simple are boring. Children are flattered by challenging demands. Challenges keep the brighter students from becoming smart alecks or reading a book or texting under their desks.

Ask questions that require critical thinking—questions that begin with how or why.

Plan activities that call for initiative and creativity.

Sometimes challenge the students to compete against the clock. For example, say, "See if you can answer all ten questions in five minutes."

Be sure they are complete. Make each lesson a complete entity that does not depend on the previous or following lesson. Some students are frequently absent, especially those who spend days at the home of their other parent. With lessons that are complete in themselves, these children will not feel left out. You might prepare summaries of your lessons and post them or email them, so that the absentees can be filled in on what they missed.

Tips for planning good lessons

Try the following for planning the best possible lessons.

- Use the manual your program provides. It offers lessons by experts that are well worked out, geared to the age level of the students, and full of good ideas.

- Begin a lesson with something that will immediately intrigue the children, such as a mysterious box, a puzzle, a joke, or a riddle. Starting lessons with an interesting activity encourages students to be on time.

- Rehearse your lessons mentally in order to plan specific directions, foresee problems, and imagine your class's reactions.

- Plan your lessons to make sure your students experience success. Students who continually fail become dissatisfied. Their negative feelings lead to problems.

- Have a back-up plan, or "ice-box plan," in case a lesson cannot be carried out, for example, if a speaker does not arrive or if you do not have time to prepare the next lesson.

- Write an outline of your plan on a card to guide you during class.

Teach a smooth, lively lesson

Once I observed a primary class in which the teacher talked for forty minutes straight, asking questions every now and then. The children were literally falling out of their seats, while I was falling asleep.

At the outset give the students a preview of what they will be doing during the lesson. Keep them apprised of the stages of the lesson so they can feel that progress is being made. Make remarks like "There is only one more section to read." Maintain a sure, brisk pace. Your tone of voice and the rate at which you speak can make the difference between bright-eyed students and sleepy ones.

Move smoothly and quickly from one activity to another with no gaps of time in which children can entertain themselves. Avoid flip-flopping or mixing lesson parts. For instance, don't make comments such as "When we were discussing page three fifteen minutes ago, I forgot to mention. . ."

In giving directions, wait until you have every student's attention. Then give clear, concise directions in as few words as possible. Otherwise you will face a barrage of questions and a room full of buzzing students trying to clarify for one another what to do. Give directions only once to train the students to listen. You might have a child repeat them. Then ask if there are any questions. Whenever directions involve a page in the book, write the page number on the board and circle it for easy reference.

Don't distribute materials until it is time to use them. Otherwise the students will play with them, read them, or be distracted while you want their undivided attention.

Ways to keep students alert

Try the following methods to keep those you teach on their toes at all times.

Come up with surprises. Award special prizes. Display an unusual object that is related to the lesson, but don't explain it until it is time. Celebrate odd events, like reaching page 100 in the textbook. Award door prizes. Introduce incongruity into the class unexpectedly to capture attention. For example, begin speaking pig-Latin, pretend to be a magician, wear a costume, or tell a short joke. Surprises help make classes fun and exciting.

Call students at random. Ask a question first and then call a name to keep all the students thinking. You might prepare a set of cards with their names, and call the names as you turn over the cards so that everyone must answer eventually. Sometimes draw a card from the back of the pile so that children who already answered must remain alert.

Try not to call on the same students all the time. You may be tempted to do this to be sure of getting a correct answer and speeding up the lesson. However, it smacks of favoritism.

To encourage the students to listen to one another, occasionally ask one of them if he or she agrees with the answer just given.

Ask the whole class to respond. Address questions for which all of the students will respond by a show of hands, by standing, or by some other gesture. For example say, "Give a thumbs up if you agree that David is a real hero and a thumbs down if you do not." At times ask the students to all give the answer to a question at once. Repeat the question until everyone is responding.

Evaluate your lessons

In the course of each lesson you teach, monitor its success. When students are restless or bored, acknowledge the fact. You might even ask them why they feel that way. Then make a change in your plan to gain their attention—even a drastic change. For example, stop reading the text and have the students stand and add gestures to a song or hold an unexpected review with rapid-fire questions.

After each class reflect on the lesson. If you had to teach the lesson again, what would you do differently? Make notes in your manual or on your written plan.

For Your Reflection

- How much time do you spend preparing your lessons? Do you feel it is enough? Why or why not?

- If you were a student in your class, how would you feel about your lesson? Be honest!

- What grade do you think those you teach would give you for your lessons? How might they grade your attitude toward them?

CHAPTER
seven

Developing Positive Attitudes

Identifying Potential Problems

Starting Off Right

Creating Your Own Techniques

Instilling Mutual Respect

Presenting Fascinating Lessons

Leaning on Others

Involving the Students

Noticing Absolutely Everything

Emphasizing the Positive

A FANCIFUL STORY relates what happened when Jesus first appeared in heaven after his death and resurrection. An angel met him and, seeing his wounds, said, "You must have suffered terribly down there. Does everyone on Earth know how much you love them?" Jesus answered, "No, just a few in a corner of Palestine. But I've asked Peter, James, John, and other apostles to tell others. Then these will tell others until everyone has heard the Good News."

But the angel knew human beings and asked, "What if the apostles forget? What if the others fail to tell about you and your sacrifice? Have you made any other plans?"

"I have no other plans," replied Jesus. "I'm counting on them."

Christianity is a religion of interdependence. Jesus counts on us to carry on his work of teaching. No matter what subject we teach, we can count on others to help us fulfill this awesome, all-important ministry.

Principals, DREs, and fellow teachers are supportive people. When you feel that your class is getting out of control, or you are at your wits' end because of a certain child's behavior, don't let pride keep you from getting assistance. Asking for help is not a sign of weakness, but indicates a desire to improve. You will be doing your students and yourself a favor. Don't wait until your class is utter chaos and unbearable. Before seeking outside help, however, make sure you have tried private talks with those who are causing you problems.

Contact parents

Your best recourse is to contact parents. Parents know their children better than we do. They are the primary educators of their children. You might set up a conference, but one phone call might make the difference. When one sixth-grade boy's behavior became intolerable, I called his mother and asked if she had any suggestions. She merely said, "Don't worry. I'll take care of this." Before the next class, the boy apologized to me and became almost a model student. When there were lapses in his behavior, I simply had to ask, "Do I have to call home again?" and he would do what was expected.

Prepare to discuss the situation with parents by taking ongoing notes on the student's behavior. Note the specific infraction and the date.

Approach parents with the attitude that together you can work to solve the problem. You may find out that they are aware of the problem already and can give you advice.

They may inform you of other factors that will shed light on the problem and help you to understand the child better. If parents are skeptical or difficult to talk to, that may be a clue to the child's behavior.

In talking to parents, be honest and don't skirt the issue. Be able to back up what you say with specific examples. Try to be tactful. Use positive expressions about their children. At the end of a phone conversation, let them hang up first.

Following are a few harsh ways to state the bald truth along with a kinder, gentle way to express it.

Negative	More positive
lazy	can do more if he or she tries
cheats	wasn't honest
rude	inconsiderate
troublemaker	disturbs the class
lies	stretches the truth
mean	has difficulty in getting along
selfish	seldom shares
shows off	tries to get attention
wastes time	could make better use of time
never does the right thing	can learn to do the right thing
often interrupts	enjoys offering his or her opinions

Hold a conference with the student and parents, thus providing an opportunity to talk about the problem. Invite the child to clarify his or her feelings and together face the situation constructively.

After parents have been involved in helping you solve a problem, contact them with feedback about how their child is improving. You might record a lesson (audio or visual) and go through it with them. This shows them you care about their child and not just his or her behavior.

Appeal to administrators

Your principal, department head, and DRE are there for you. They will be glad to help. Consult them about your discipline problems. Invite them into your class to observe or to teach a lesson for you.

You might tape a lesson (audio or video) and analyze it with them. The source of your problem may be an annoying mannerism you are not even aware of and that could be easily eliminated from your teaching.

Send misbehaving children to administrators for help in solving the problem, not for punishment. Try to take care of your own punishments. Be aware that sending children to the principal or DRE might weaken your students' regard for you.

Use peer support

Your colleagues will sympathize with you and support you. Ask them for advice and be willing to share with them what has worked for you. Talk out frustrations with a coworker, one who can give sound advice as well as boost your morale. He or she might share horror stories that top your own!

Visit the classes of other teachers or catechists. By observing good teachers, you will glean tricks of the trade for maintaining discipline. You will also develop a sense for the friendly but businesslike style of teaching that creates a healthy atmosphere.

A priest or a counselor may be able to help you cope with discipline problems and offer advice. Your own family members, who probably know you through and through, can possibly give you insight into your discipline problems.

Sometimes you will be able to enlist the help of other students to guide a student to better behavior. A few days after school started, John, a first-grader, cried for his mommy and refused to go into the classroom. The principal called for a first-grade boy who had cried on the first day. She asked him, "Remember how you had a hard time leaving your mother? What could John do?" The boys sat on the steps. The second boy counseled John, "We have to do work, and your mommy has to do work. So let's get to work." Then the two boys got up and walked into the classroom.

An appeal to the whole class for their opinion of a misdeed is effective in stopping it when you don't know who the guilty person is.

Attend lectures and read books and magazines that provide information on being a good teacher and suggestions for discipline. A marvelous book is *You Can Handle Them All* written by Robert L. LeBruyn and Jack L. Larson. This handbook describes more than one hundred problem behaviors and recommends specific techniques for handling each one. It is published by The Master Teacher, Inc. (Leadership Lane, P.O. Box 1207; Manhattan, KS 66502) and can be found at www.masterteacher.com

Call on God

Finally, rely on the Holy Spirit for help. You might wish to adopt or compose a special prayer to tap into supernatural power before each class. Here is a sample:

Holy Spirit, be with me as I share in the work of Jesus. Let the truths I teach sink into the minds and hearts of my students. May they come to know your love, follow your way, and be good and productive citizens. Amen.

One fifth-grade boy was incorrigible. No one could control him. Repeatedly teachers and playground supervisors sent him to the principal. Finally the principal said to him one day, "We have tried so hard to teach you to have good behavior. I don't know what else to do. I guess I'm just going to have to talk to Jesus about you." Then and there the principal spoke aloud to Jesus, asking his help in changing the boy's conduct. Miraculously, that solved the problem.

Trust God to draw good out of your disasters. A colleague counseled me one day: "Remember that you are an instrument of God. The Holy Spirit is acting in you to touch their lives in ways that you may never know. Trust God, do your best, and don't worry."

Pray for your students as well as for yourself. One wise teacher advised, "Spend more time talking to God about your students than you spend talking to your students about God."

Keep children's names in your prayer book or in your plan book. Before preparing a lesson, pray for the children individually—each of them, the nice and the naughty. Praying for your students may change your attitude if nothing else, and that could make all the difference in the world.

For Your Reflection

- What can you do to remind yourself that you do not teach alone but with God's help? Which of the suggestions in this chapter would work best for you?

- To whom could you go for help with discipline? Have you tried talking to your principal or DRE? Have you sought advice from veteran teachers? If not, resolve to do so as soon as possible.

- Do you ever go directly to parents when you have a problem? Why or why not? What has been the result?

CHAPTER
eight

D eveloping Positive Attitudes

I dentifying Potential Problems

S tarting Off Right

C reating Your Own Techniques

I nstilling Mutual Respect

P resenting Fascinating Lessons

L eaning on Others

I nvolving the Students

N oticing Absolutely Everything

E mphasizing the Positive

Most students are less likely to cause trouble if they have a sense of belonging and ownership and if they are kept busy. Involving children in activities fills both of these needs. In addition, activities promote learning. Supposedly students remember only twenty percent of what they hear but eighty percent of what they do.

Invite participation in class planning

Give those you teach a say in setting the standards for the class or for certain activities. Before a group discussion, for instance, ask them to propose guidelines to follow and appoint a secretary to list these at the board.

Offer a choice of activities: "Do you want to watch a video or put on a play?" "Would you rather write a report or give an oral report?" Also give children choices in minor matters. Ask "Do you wish to work alone or in groups, in pencil or pen, on colored paper or white?"

Keep children active

Channel your students' natural tendencies and characteristic energy to accomplish your lesson's goals. Hold activities that require talking: discussions, group work, and art projects. Invite questions and comments during the lesson. Be careful, though, that the children don't often sidetrack you so that the lesson's objectives are not achieved.

Never tell children something they can tell you. Instead of giving a summary of a paragraph, ask them for one. Instead of reviewing what was studied in the last lesson, let them do it. After you pose a question, allow sufficient "think time" and be comfortable with the silence instead of answering the question yourself.

Incorporate activities that engage those you teach in other kinds of physical activity such as singing, walking to the board, putting on plays, role-playing, racing, and making something.

Never do something that the students can do, even if you think you can do it faster or better. Let them pass out papers, write or draw a picture on the board, read from the Bible, and manage the audiovisual technology. Having children operate the equipment frees you to supervise the class better.

If the students are reading their text, direct them to highlight keywords, underline sentences, star ideas, number facts, and jot notes in the margins as they go along. Occasionally let individual children be the teacher for a while. You will see yourself reflected in their voices and style of teaching.

Try cooperative learning

Cooperative learning worked for me when I taught a class of "low-track" freshmen. At a teacher-parent conference, I learned that one ninth-grader, Martha, was a headache for all of her teachers except me. That year I was experimenting with group work. Each week my students chose activities from a list and worked together to carry them out. In this setting, Martha blossomed. One day I even overheard her scolding the others in her group, "Quiet! I want to do this."

Occasionally, plan for cooperative learning. Let the students work with partners (buddy study) or in groups. You might make each group responsible for teaching something to the whole class. Or find a project for the students to work on together, perhaps a parish activity. An added advantage of cooperative learning is that it teaches skills and virtues that are basic for the Christian community.

By the way, when two children have a disagreement or a fight and disrupt the class, have them talk to each other until they can settle their disagreement. Encourage and advise them as they work to find a solution to their problem, but don't do it for them.

Employ conflict resolution methods

Principals and teachers find conflict resolution methods and mediation methods very effective in diffusing situations that involve two or more angry students. Teachers trained in these methods function as peacemakers rather than enforcers. In addition, children learn to handle their problems in a mature and Christian way.

At one school, the junior-high students were upset because a girl threatened to beat up another girl at a school dance. The principal brought the two girls together and worked through the process of mediation with happy results. Of their own accord, after leaving the office, the two girls visited each junior-high class and apologized for the trouble they had caused. Moreover, afterwards the aggressor made it a point to tell the principal how much she had enjoyed the dance.

The following steps of conflict resolution are adapted from one successful method. (*Conflict Resolution: An Elementary School Curriculum*, reprinted with permission by the Community Board Program, 1540 Market Street, San Francisco, California, 94102, chapter 6, ©1990).

1. Both students agree on three ground rules: Each one states, "I agree not to interrupt, not to name call, and to work to resolve the conflict."

2. One person tells his or her side of the story using statements that begin with "I," not "you." He or she includes how he or she feels and what he or she wants.

3. The second person restates what the first person said. He or she may begin with "So the problem for you is. . . ." and may ask questions to understand the situation better.

4. The second person tells his or her side of the story using "I-messages."

5. The first person restates what the second person said and may ask questions.

6. Both persons suggest solutions that will help both.

7. The students work to agree on a resolution that is

   • specific, with all the details spelled out

   • balanced, so that both people share the responsibility for making it work

   • realistic

   • and solves the problem and addresses the underlying issue.

In preparation for the meeting, the students might fill out forms on which they complete statements like "I have a problem with. . ." and "Two solutions for my problem are. . ."

In mediating between two young children, the steps can be shortened to these three:

1. Each child says how he or she feels, what happened, and what he or she wants.
2. Each student suggests something he or she can do to solve the problem.
3. The students work together to agree on a resolution.

Often it is sufficient to have the young victim tell how he or she felt when an incident occurred and then ask the other child how he or she feels now. Most likely the little offender will immediately express regret.

You might investigate local teacher-training courses in conflict resolution and mediation.

Include everyone

Make it a point to call on every student during class. Match the level of question to the ability of the students so that the less gifted ones can answer correctly and experience success.

When speaking to the class, look at the students, not down at the floor, at a spot above their heads, or at a few select students. Avoid favoritism. It will turn the class against you.

After an activity, ask the students to comment on their behavior and how it could be improved. Periodically assess together how the goals set at the beginning of the year are being met.

For Your Reflection

- What things have you been doing in class that students would be able to do?

- What topics in your curriculum lend themselves to cooperative learning? Have you already experimented with this type of learning? With what result?

- Do you try to keep children as active as possible as they go through your lessons? What techniques work for you? Which activities do your students enjoy?

CHAPTER
nine

Developing Positive Attitudes

Identifying Potential Problems

Starting Off Right

Creating Your Own Techniques

Instilling Mutual Respect

Presenting Fascinating Lessons

Leaning on Others

Involving the Students

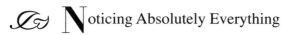Noticing Absolutely Everything

Emphasizing the Positive

THE COMMENT ABOUT TEACHERS HAVING EYES in the back of their heads is not farfetched. A good teacher tries to see and hear everything that's going on. Make sure, though, that you really see what you think you see and interpret it correctly. Avoid jumping to conclusions. Once, while teaching class, out of the corner of my eye I saw two people disappear through the forbidden door in the hall that led to the roof. Having caught two students the day before dropping erasers off that roof onto the children below, I ran to the door and called out, "Just where do you think you're going?" Two men appeared and introduced themselves as diocesan official surveying the building! They eased my embarrassment by praising my vigilance.

Always try to be observant

We can be so engrossed in our lesson that we fail to notice things like Larry's setting fire to Jim's pants with a lighter. Being well prepared for class frees us to give more attention to those we teach. When our eyes aren't glued to our manual or plan, we can glance around the class and make eye contact where necessary.

Stand while teaching in order to have a better view of the class. Periodically scan the class as you teach. Circulate among the children during a lesson. This will keep you in touch with what's happening and will squelch many an unwelcome activity. It will also force the students to turn their heads and move their eyes. If you always teach behind a desk or lectern, both you and the children will quickly become bored.

Here are other ways you can be observant:

- If you don't dare turn your back on your class to write on the board, use an overhead projector or a projector and a whiteboard.

- Always look ahead. If an upcoming lesson, a prayer service, or a movie includes a section that will induce puzzlement, consternation, or a strong reaction in your students, prepare them for it.

- Try to deal with more than one issue at a time. Observing how adroit you are at doing two acts simultaneously, students are less apt to disrupt the learning process with misbehavior. They'll know you can handle them.

- Stop undesirable activity immediately, nonverbally if possible. If it continues, other students will soon imitate the activity and your problems will increase.

- When students are doing independent or group work, keep an eye on them. Better still, be with them. Just because they are occupied, don't use this time to prepare your next lesson or to read a novel at your desk.

Overlook things (sometimes)

At times there are good reasons to ignore misbehavior during class. Maybe the "crime" is not serious, and stopping to take note of it will cause more disruption than ignoring it. Also, your calling attention to it might be just what the child wants. Creating a scene would give him or her attention, but it might also damage the learning process.

You may need more time to evaluate the situation. Besides, a problem that seems like a disaster at the end of a hard day can shrink to molehill size after a rest. Weigh all the factors and use good judgment in determining whether or not it is worthwhile to correct a student during class, should the same behavior come up again.

Apply whenever possible the motto of Saint Pope John XXIII: "See everything. Overlook much. Correct a little."

Make notes regularly

It's important to take notes about what you observe as you teach. Try to make a habit of doing this after each class. Sometimes what you observe may give you insights about something you are doing wrong. If you notice that your students often seem bored and unresponsive, you may need to vary your activities.

If you notice that the behavior of a particular student has changed from friendly to withdrawn, you may want to contact his or her parents. If you're not observant, you won't even notice the change.

If you are aware that a certain child is often the cause of disruptions during your lessons, you will want to note this and the circumstances so that you are prepared to describe or explain this behavior to parents as well as to help the child. Be objective. Record specific and significant offenses and the dates on a 3" x 5" file card.

Evaluate each lesson

Evaluate each lesson to become more aware of what went right and what went wrong and why. Consider how you handled individual cases of misbehavior. Determine ways you can improve.

For Your Reflection

- How can you become more aware of what is going on in your class? What do you do now to keep aware?

- Are you willing to overlook minor problems sometimes? Why or why not?

- Do you regularly make notes for improving a lesson? Do you keep track of students' major infractions in your class? If not, how could you begin?

CHAPTER
ten

Developing Positive Attitudes

Identifying Potential Problems

Starting Off Right

Creating Your Own Techniques

Instilling Mutual Respect

Presenting Fascinating Lessons

Leaning on Others

Involving the Students

Noticing Absolutely Everything

Emphasizing the Positive

The observation of Saint Francis de Sales, "You can catch more flies with a drop of honey than with a barrel of vinegar" holds true in the classroom. When I was a ninth-grader, one day after I finished sweeping the classroom floor my teacher remarked, "This floor is so clean you could eat off it." That comment made me feel proud—and determined to be the best floor sweeper ever for the rest of the year.

Reinforce good behavior

Be generous in giving "a pat on the back." Positive words have positive reactions. Children love to be praised. So do adults for that matter. The man responsible for the art and design of textbooks I was writing appreciated the positive comments I jotted on the page proofs. He cut them out and pinned them to the bulletin board in his office! Be lavish with praise but not dishonest. Children know when praise is deserved and when it is insincere praise used as a ploy.

Praise indicates success, which is the best motivator, and stimulates students to continue trying. Also, complimenting one child or a small group prods the rest of the class to imitate the behavior that was praised. Make a comment like, "How hard the boys and girls in the third row are working" and watch how children in rows one, two, four, and five immediately settle down.

Give attention and praise to those students who are doing the right thing and ignore those who are not. Unrewarded behaviors become extinct.

Occasionally comment on the entire class's good behavior. For example, say, "I like the way everyone followed directions." Be sure to praise the class when they have not been influenced by the misbehavior of one or a few students.

Here are some ways to offer praise.

- Give verbal praise before, during, and after class.

- Make it a habit to write positive comments on students' work. A "nice job" or "good thinking" at the top of a paper is worth the extra time and effort it takes to write.

- Phone students at home to praise them for good behavior you noticed in your class. Or call or e-mail a student's parents about something positive he or she has done. They will be pleasantly surprised.

- Write a little note on special paper or a card to congratulate a student for good behavior or for a noticeable improvement.

- Display the students' work in the room and in the parish hall.

- Ask to keep some papers or artwork. The students will be pleased and proud.

In addition to praise, use other incentives for good behavior. Give out stars, stickers, and other small rewards. Bestow privileges or let the children do something they like to do. One teacher had an old, scarred student desk in her room and was reluctant to assign it to any child. Then she had a brilliant idea. She dubbed the ugly desk "the honor desk," and the student whose behavior was outstanding was permitted to sit in it the following week!

Make a large cardboard badge that has the initials RTG for Real Third Grader (or initials for the grade you teach). Cover the badge with clear contact paper and tape a safety pin on the back. As a quick alternate, use a plastic name badge with RTG (or other initials) in place of the name. At the end of each class or week, award the badge to a student to take home. Specify what the student did to deserve the badge. Stress that he or she must remember to return the badge for the next class.

Educational psychologists estimate that the ratio of negative teacher comments to positive ones is 8 to 1. Record one of your lessons. As you replay it, keep score on paper how many of your statements were positive and how many were negative. Note missed opportunities to give your students a boost.

Be positive about yourself

Know that your ministry is challenging. Actor Dick Van Dyke once described a teacher in words similar to these:

> A teacher must have the faith of Abraham,
> the patience of Job,
> the wisdom of Solomon,
> the courage of Daniel as he goes into the lions' den,
> and the confidence of Moses that it is all worthwhile.

Evaluate yourself as a disciplinarian and notice small triumphs. Give yourself little rewards for accomplishments.

Make a Booster Box for yourself as a morale builder. Save tokens of your successes, such as thank-you notes from your students or parents and words of praise from colleagues. In hard times go through your collection and recall that you are good and doing a fine job.

Keep things in perspective. Know that your students aren't miniature adults. Also realize that not everyone is your class is delinquent. Focus on those students who are receptive and teach to them so that your efforts won't seem in vain, and you will be motivated to go on.

If you have an "impossible" class, if the principal or DRE is afraid to come into your room, and if other teachers refer to your class as "wild animals," persevere. Muster reserve supplies of enthusiasm and hide your feelings of defeat. A sense of humor may save you, whereas breaking down before the students in rage or in tears of frustration puts the reins of control firmly in their hands.

Learn to take criticism

Take criticism from students and parents with a grain of salt. Look for objective proof. Once during a phone call with a mother whose daughter was a classroom menace, I was told: "Ann and her friends say you favor the Black students." That very night I was at a parent conference for a Black girl in the same class, and her mother charged, "You are known to pick on the Black students."

If you come prepared to do your best and don't take the class's failures as personal failures, you will manage to be at peace. Remember, your students' bad behavior is not against you personally, but against your authority role. Seldom is the behavior meant to hurt you. Someday you may laugh at these experiences. In the meantime, make yourself a sign that says, "This too shall pass!"

Whatever you do, don't quit. You have a lot to offer, and the Church needs you.

Enjoy your job

Being a teacher can be an enjoyable and fulfilling ministry. If you are finding it a chore or a burden and can hardly wait until class is over each time, figure out why. It may be that you are doing too much and do not have the time to be a successful teacher. Or perhaps you would be better working with a different grade level. Maybe a change in content would be good.

Take whatever measures you can to be a joyful, dedicated Christian. If you are not happy in the classroom, the students will sense this and problems will develop. When you are tempted to get discouraged, remember these words of Saint Paul to young Saint Timothy (paraphrased):

Your role is so important. I implore you to continue to proclaim God's Word. Be persistent in your teaching whether it is convenient or inconvenient. Do everything you can to convince, reprimand, and encourage children to hear the truth. Above all, be very patient with them.

—2 Timothy 4:2

For Your Reflection

- Would you consider yourself a negative or positive teacher? Why do you think this is so?

- Do you tend to focus on the difficult aspects of your ministry or the positive ones? Have you ever tried the "Booster Box" suggestion?

- How do you react to Saint Paul's words to Saint Timothy?

- Do you pray for a joyful heart? Why not start today?

CONCLUSION

As I write this, the world is preparing for the Summer Olympics in Rio de Janeiro, Brazil. We will witness the fruit of many years of discipline on the part of those champions competing for medals. Saint Paul reminds us, "Athletes exercise self-control in all things; they do it to receive a perishable wreath, but we an imperishable one" (1 Corinthians 9:25). As teachers, we practice discipline as we try to instill discipline in those we teach. After all, we are going for the gold. We are determined to be good teachers who form new generations of knowledgeable, dedicated Christians on fire with love for God and others. We are willing to give our all in carrying out our mission.

We are convinced of the importance of imparting to our children the values, morals, and virtues needed to live happily and to heal this world's wounds. These crucial goals as well as our ultimate goal—our own salvation—motivate and energize us. And the means to attain these goals is discipline, our own and our students'.

Not an easy task

Of course, our task is difficult and demanding—even more so than balancing on a high beam. Jesus never said that sharing his message would be easy. Instead he talked about being insulted and persecuted, taking up the cross, shaking dust off our feet from towns that rejected his teaching, and being sent like sheep in the midst of wolves! At times we feel overwhelmed and discouraged.

Thinking we are not accomplishing anything, we are tempted to quit. Especially at these times it is good to remember that we are only called to do our best—and then leave the rest up to God. In the end we all must echo Saint Paul's words: "I planted, Apollos watered, but God gave the growth" (1 Corinthians 3:6). It is God who is the real coach.

If you are a beginning teacher or catechist, you might be wondering how you will ever be able to put into practice everything in this book. I recommend concentrating on one or two chapters a year, beginning with chapter 2, "Starting Off Right." With time, experience, and little help from friends, you will probably develop into a master teacher.

Beatitudes for teachers

In the meantime, as you practice the fine art of discipline, you might ponder the following Beatitudes for teachers. They recap some of the main concepts in this book:

Happy are the organized and prepared, for their lessons will run smoothly, leaving no time for the students to get into mischief or even to think about it.

Happy are the creative, careful lesson planners, for they will hold their students' attention and their classes will not be boring.

Happy are the observing and alert, for they will be aware of their class's moods and activities and prevent many problems.

HAPPY ARE THE LOVING, CARING TEACHERS, for their students will try not to disappoint them.

HAPPY ARE THE FIRM AND FAIR, for they will listen and be listened to.

HAPPY ARE THOSE WHO DISCIPLINE WITH RESPECT for the children, for respect will be given them.

HAPPY ARE THOSE WHO TEACH WITH ENTHUSIASM, for their students will catch their spirit and grow in knowledge and faith.

HAPPY ARE TEACHERS WHO CONTINUE TO LEARN, for so will their students—with peace, joy, and satisfaction.

May this book help you to carry out your significant role in the Church and may it also help you to fulfill these words:

"You will shine in the world like bright stars because you are offering it the word of life."

—Philippians 2:15 (Jerusalem Bible)

ABOUT THE AUTHOR

Mary Kathleen Glavich, SND, from Cleveland, Ohio, after teaching every grade from first to twelfth, became an award-winning author and an international speaker. She worked on several textbook series and has written more than eighty books on faith formation including a novel, *The Fisherman's Wife: The Gospel According to St. Peter's Spouse*. She blogs at www.kathleenglavich.org.